# Vahram's Chronicl

# Armenian kingdom in Cilicia,

# during the time of the Crusades

Vahram

(Translator: Karl Friedrich Neumann)

**Alpha Editions**

This edition published in 2024

ISBN : 9789362095220

Design and Setting By
**Alpha Editions**
www.alphaedis.com
Email - info@alphaedis.com

# Contents

# PREFACE.

The greatest defect of the following Chronicle is its brevity. VAHRAM, of whose life little more is known than that he was a native of Edessa, a priest, and the secretary of king Leon III., exhibits almost all the faults of the common Chroniclers of the Middle Ages. He relates many barren facts, without stating the circumstances with which they were connected, and he mistakes every where the passions of men for the finger of God. The compilers of chronicles were in those ages ignorant of the true end, and unacquainted with the proper objects of history. But with all its defects, the chronicle of the Armenian kings of Cilicia, written by a contemporary writer, is valuable. The friend of history may now be enabled to form an estimate of the origin and the increase of an empire, which for want of materials has been overlooked by the most learned and acute historians. Gibbon, of whom it is doubtful whether we should most admire his genius or his erudition, in his celebrated work simply mentions the *name* of Cilicia, a kingdom, which carried on successful wars against the emperors of Constantinople; and which, from the beginning of the Crusades remained the friend and ally of the Franks, and to whom belonged a part of the sea-coast, that continued from the time of Ezekiel the theatre of the commerce of the world. The Venetians and Genoese were so impressed with the importance of Cilicia, that they made several commercial treaties with the Armenian kings; the Armenian original of one of these agreements, together with a translation and notes, has been printed by the learned orientalist, Saint-Martin.

The Crusaders were astonished to find within the frontiers of the Byzantine empire a powerful prince and ally of whom they had never before heard mention. Nicetas betrays a want of historical knowledge and research, in saying that the Armenians and Germans were united together, because they both disliked holy images.[1] The Germans and a great part of the Armenians, on the contrary, felt no aversion to the worship of images, but the latter, ever since the first division of the Arsacidian kingdom of Armenia between the Sassanides and the Greeks, in the year three hundred and eighty-seven, had been in perpetual warfare with the Byzantine empire; and this warfare caused a degree of animosity between the two people (Greeks and Armenians), of which traces may be seen even at the present time.

By the unjust and cruel division of the kingdom of Armenia, the largest and most fertile part of the country fell (as the contemporary historian Lazar of Barb observes) to the empire of Persia. The Byzantine emperors and the Sassanian princes for a while permitted native kings to hold a precarious sceptre; but they were speedily dismissed; and the Byzantine part of Armenia was governed by a Greek magistrate, and the Persian by a Marsban or

Margrave. This state of the country, somewhat similar to that of the Maronites in our times, was on a sudden changed by the conquests of the Arabs; but the Armenians would not accept the Koran, and their condition became worse under the zealous and fanatical followers of the prophet of Mecca than under the descendants of Sapor the Great, while weak and dismayed by civil wars.

Ashod the Bagratide, an Armenian nobleman of a Jewish family, who had fled to Armenia after the destruction of Jerusalem by Nebuchadanozor, at last gained the confidence of his Arabian masters; and in the year eight hundred and fifty-nine was appointed Emir al Omra, Ishkhan Ishkhanaz (prince of princes),—as the native historians translate the Arabian title—over all Armenia: and was soon after it (888) favoured with a tributary crown. The Bagratides and the rival kings of the family of the Arzerounians, were the faithful friends (or slaves) of the Arabs, and often suffered from the inroads and devastations of the Greeks. We learn from Vahram the means through which the Bagratian kingdom in Armenia Proper was extinguished; and that a new Armenian kingdom arose on the craggy rocks of Mount Taurus, and which gradually extended its boundaries to the sea-coast, including the whole province of Cilicia. Vahram carries his monotonous historical rhymes no farther down than the time of the death of his sovereign, Leon III. (1289); but the Cilicio-Armenian kingdom, which during the whole time of its existence perhaps never was entirely independent, lasted nearly a hundred years longer. Leon, the sixth of that name and the last Armenian king of Cilicia, was in 1375 taken a prisoner by the Mamalukes of Egypt, and after a long captivity (1382) released by the generous interference of King John I. of Castille. He was not however permitted to return to his own country; but wandered through Europe from one country to another till his death, which happened at Paris, the 19th of November 1393. He was buried in the monastery of the Celestines.

The Mamalukes did not long remain masters both of Cilicia and of a part of Armenia Proper; but yielded to the fortune and the strength of the descendants of Osman or Othman: when the Armenians again felt, as in former times, all the disasters to which the frontier provinces between two rival empires are usually exposed. The cruel policy of the Sophies transplanted thousands of Christian families to the distant provinces of Persia, and transformed fertile provinces into artificial deserts. The Armenians therefore, like the Jews, were obliged to disperse themselves over the world, and resort to commerce for the necessaries of life. Armenian merchants are now to be found in India, on the islands of the Eastern Archipelago, in Singapore, in Afghanistan, Persia, Egypt, in every part of Asia Minor and Syria, Russia, Poland, Austria, Italy; and even the present patriarch of Abyssinia is an Armenian. The valiant descendants of Haig are now, like the offspring of Abraham, considered every where clever and shrewd merchants: they were of great service to the East-India Company in carrying on their trade with the inland provinces of Hindostan; and it was once thought that they were fitter for this part of the mercantile business, than any agents of the Company itself.[2]

It is not more than half a century since the modern Armenian provinces began to look on Russia for succour and relief, when the Empress Catherine behaved in many instances most generously to the ruined house of Thorgoma. The fortunate wars of Russia against the Shah and the Sultan have within the last ten years brought the greater part of the old Parthian kingdom of Armenia under the sway of the mighty Czars. It seems probable, that we may see yet in our times a new kingdom of Armenia, created out of barbarian elements by the generosity and magnanimity of the Emperor Nicholas.

The following Chronicle is translated from an edition printed at Madras in the year 1259 of the Armenian era, that is the year 1810 *Anno Domini.* The volume is printed by the command of that great promoter of literature, Ephrem, archbishop and primate of the Armenians in Russia, and contains, besides the chronicle of Vahram, the Elegy of Edessa by Nerses Shnorhaly; and the elegy on his death, written by the most eminent of his disciples, Nerses of Lampron. It is said in the preface of the before-mentioned volume, that the work of Vahram, the secretary of Leon III., had been previously printed, though in a very negligent and careless manner. I have never however seen any other than the Madras edition, where the proper names of places and foreign nations are often incorrectly spelt. I am sorry to add, that I made the following translation in a place where it was impossible for me to refer to the well known works on the geography of Armenia, of Cilicia, and of Asia Minor generally; neither could I compare the narrative of Vahram with the statements of the contemporary Byzantine and Latin writers: but I trust the learned reader will easily supply these defects.

Vahram is nearly the latest author who is considered by the Armenian literati to write classically. The classical Armenian language had been preserved from the beginning of Armenian literature in the fifth century, amidst various political and religious disturbances, for a period of eight hundred years. During the course of the thirteenth century the language became corrupted; and in the fourteenth authors began to use in their writings the corrupted vernacular idiom. The ancient native writers were neglected, their classical translations and imitations of the celebrated Greek patterns became superseded by the barbarous literature of the Latins, and John of Erzinga, otherwise Bluz (1326), the last who wrote the language of Moses and Elisæus, translated a work on the sacraments by St. Thomas Aquinas.

We thus find some orders of monks in Armenia, educated in the Latin schools and in latin manners, who corrupted the native Haican language by the introduction of many foreign scholastic expressions; and a new race of sanguinary barbarians, the Dominicans, became the authors of works worthy of their titulary saint. The Armenian literature remained in this abject condition, to which these holy fathers had reduced it, for nearly four hundred years; but about the middle of the eighteenth century the nation roused itself from this lethargy, and Madras, Calcutta, Djulfa, New Nakshivan, Etshmiadsin, Tabris, St. Petersburg, Moscow, Amsterdam, Smyrna, and principally Venice, bear witness to the literary energy of the far dispersed descendants of Haig. With the dawn of Armenian literature, history has been enriched by the Chronicle of Eusebius; yet more and weightier literary treasures may be expected from its meridian splendour. There are hints in the writers of the fifth century, of translations of Polybius, Diodorus Siculus, and the Chronicle of Julius Africanus. Besides these versions of the classical writers of Greece, there exist very valuable original histories, which have never been printed or translated, and many a chasm might be filled up in the history of the middle ages by these authors. We should, perhaps, be introduced to nations now totally lost, or so mingled with others, that it is impossible to distinguish them. There is a rumour of a manuscript history of the Albanians,—a nation well known to Strabo and to Moses of Chorene,[3] said to exist at a monastery in Armenia Proper,—of those Albanians, who lived between Iberia or Georgia and the confines of the Caspian Sea; but of which people no traces are to be found in our times.

A literary journey to Armenia, undertaken by an active laborious scholar, who unites the knowledge of the Armenian language with classical studies, would prove of the greatest importance to the knowledge of ancient history and to the advancement of general literature.

---

# THE CHRONICLE.

The Patriarch Nerses, called the Gracious,(1) has written a history of Armenia in verse, informing us of the manners and customs of our forefathers, from the highest antiquity down to his own time; and by so doing he admonished the people to walk in the path of righteousness. Seeing and reading this history, Leon, the anointed king of Armenia,(2) has been pleased to command me, the poor in spirit, to subjoin to the work of our holy father both what has been reported by faithful witnesses, and what we have seen with our own eyes. And he commanded me to write this supplement (also in verse), that it may be read with more pleasure.(3)

Now I, Raboun Vahram, am convinced of my want of talents, but am well versed in the law of God, and have never deviated from the path of righteousness. Receiving the commands of the king, I have been ever since uneasy in my mind, out of fear that in not obeying, I may bring on me the two-fold punishment spoken of by St. Paul.(4) For, if to subjoin my mean composition to those of the ancients be audacious, to think that it could be compared with their finished productions, would be folly. This alarmed me, and I abstained from writing. Considering this very seriously, I thought at last that my humble and mean writing would increase the beauty of others, to which it was subjoined: the same as painters intentionally surround a gold ground by a black colour, not to adorn this black border, but to raise the beauty of the gold.(5) These considerations made me regain confidence, and I felt resolution enough to undertake this work. I confide in Him, whose grace is unbounded, who knows what nobody has seen, who under three appearances is only of one nature, *Father*, *Son*, and *Holy Ghost*; whose reign is for ever, who alone should be worshipped, and who alone creates and preserves all beings. With his name I begin, and with his name I will finish. Both the Son and the Holy Ghost proceeded from the Father.(6) Going back a little to former times, I will give (till I come to our age), in a cursory manner, what has been written down by our forefathers.

The Christian nations have been favoured with the inheritance of God; they have been enlightened by the faith, and had excellent laws; but they strayed from those laws, and were polluted by their bad works. The measure of their sins being filled, it excited the wrath of the Lord, and a burning fire arose in the desert of Arabia called Mahomed, the son of darkness.(7) This Father of heresy drew many after him; he arose and preached by the sabre and the sword, and subdued many countries. The wickedness remained after the death of the wicked, the son followed the father, and the usurpation was confirmed.

Togrul Beg. 1037 In the course of the following centuries, the nations, whom we call Turks, came (divided into twenty-four tribes)(8) from the north, conquered the realm of Persia and adhered to the heresy of Mohamed; they humbled the kings and vanquished the emperor;(9) they filled the world with their victories and destroyed its inhabitants, endangering both body and soul of their captives.(10) They came at last to Babylon,(11) and there erecting the seat of their empire, they marched to the westward, 1042 came to Armenia, dealt hardly with its inhabitants, and laid a heavy yoke on them.(12)

Tired of this oppression, and unable to sustain all the hardships which the barbarians laid on them, the inhabitants preferred being strangers in foreign countries to remaining slaves in their own home; they left the land of their forefathers, and fled to the western and northern regions. Cakig II, the anointed king of Armenia, considering these disastrous circumstances, and the dire necessity of the case, 1045 gave up his country to the Roman Emperor, in exchange for the great and celebrated town of Cæsarea, and other places in Cappadocia; and in consequence of this, the Armenians lived as emigrants under the Greeks.(13)

But the jealousy which had existed for so many centuries between the two nations, was rooted too deep in the heart of every individual, and caused many disorders. The metropolitan of Cæsarea, named Marcus, had a dog, whom he called Armen.(14) Cakig hearing of this, 1079 invited Marcus to dinner, and asked of him the name of the dog: the frightened metropolitan called the dog by another name, the animal did not hear; but as soon as he called him by the proper name, *Armen*, the dog ran to him. The king then gave orders that both the metropolitan and his dog should be put into one sack together, and tortured until they could bear it no longer. As soon as the Greeks heard this news, they rose against the Armenians; and the sons of one Mandal killed the King Cakig.(15) This discouraged the chieftains and the leaders of the army, they ran away and were scattered over various parts of the world. A famous chief of the blood royal, *Rouben* by name, baron of the fort Kosidar,(16) hearing the news of the king's death, fled with his whole family to Mount Taurus,(17a) descended then the mountains on the other side of Phrygia, and 1080 took possession of a place called *Korhmoloss*, and remained there. Many other Armenians also took refuge in these mountains; the great Rouben united them together, and so increased his strength, that he could 1095 take possession of the whole mountain district, expel the Greeks, and secure the country for himself. He lived a holy life, and was at last raised to Christ.

*Constantine* (or Costantin, as the Armenians write the name), the son of Rouben, succeeded him in the principality,(17b) and was a valiant and magnanimous prince; his principal place was Vahga, where he had his residence, and from whence he governed his dominions. He fought many battles, and conquered many forts; he destroyed the armies of the Greeks, and took many captives. The dominions of Constantine extended to the sea;(18) he was highly honoured by the Franks, and was their ally against the Turks; they raised his possessions to the dignity of a comitatus, or county, and appointed him the Count and Margrave.(19) Valiant, kind and benevolent, and a true believer, his fame reached to the other side of the sea; he cultivated the country and rebuilt the towns, and all was blooming and cheerful during his lifetime. There occurred a sign from heaven, announcing the death of this extraordinary man; the meat brought to him on a silver plate started suddenly away, and fled to the corner of the house and hid itself among the poultry. Wise men looked on this as a sign that the king would soon be gathered to his forefathers, and so it happened. He reposeth in Christ with his father Rouben, and was buried in the church called Castalon.(20)

Constantine had two sons, the elder, who 1100 succeeded his father, was called Thoros, and the younger Leon. Thoros superabounded in wisdom, and his military valour is highly spoken of. He sought to revenge the blood of Cakig the Great, and made war against the sons of Mandal; he reduced their fort Centerhasg,(21) killed the inhabitants, and carried away great booty. He found in this place a likeness of the Holy Virgin, and treated it with great esteem: by this he became more and more powerful, and vanquished the Greeks many times. He took Anazarbus, built therein a large church, and adorned it with the names of his generals and with the likeness of the Holy Virgin. He governed valiantly, and so much was he esteemed that Cilicia lost its proper name, and has been called *The Country of Thoros*. Thoros loved God with all his heart, favoured his servants, built churches, and held the convents in high esteem, in particular those which are called *Trassarg* and *Mashgevar*; he bestowed on these and on others many gifts. Living such a holy life, he went at last in to the Lord, 1123 and was buried in the holy church called Trassarg.(22)

After the death of Thoros, his only son and heir was cast into prison by some wicked people, who administered to him a poisonous drug,(23) thus the principality came to Leon, the brother of Thoros, and his equal in reputation. *Leon* conquered Mamestia and Tarsus;(24) he invited many famous warriors to join him, and allured them by great rewards. Forward in battle, he prepared himself, and often fought against the foreigners or infidels,(25) took their forts and put all the inhabitants to the sword. He was the admiration of warriors, and the fear of foreigners or infidels, so that they called him the new *Ashtahag.*(26) After his return with honours and fame to his own country, four sons were born to him, so incomparable among men; the first was called *Thoros* the Great, who was adorned by Stephanus (or the crown). Next to Stephanus came *Meleh*, and then *Rouben.*

The Roman Emperor (Calo-Johanes), who had the surname of Porphyrogenitus,(27) hearing all that Leon had done, became very angry. He assembled a great army and brought them down into Cilicia. Leon, finding that he was surrounded by a large army, lost all confidence in his forts and fled to the mountains; but he was speedily taken and brought in fetters before the emperor. There are some who even affirm that the emperor broke his oath, and took Leon by fraud. His two sons were also arrested, and with their father carried into captivity; 1137 they were detained together in prison in Constantinople. Meleh and Stephanus were fortunately not in Cilicia at the time their father was taken prisoner; they were on a visit in Urha or Edessa, with their uncle, the count of that place.(28)

The Armenian army was destroyed, and the emperor took possession of Cilicia; he left a part of his soldiers in that country and then returned to Constantinople. The eye which looks down from heaven on the earth below had pity upon Leon and his two unfortunate sons, and the emperor's heart turned to clemency. He honoured Leon exceedingly, and gave permission to his children to stay with their father; he invited him to dinner, and permitted him the recreation of hunting; he gave him handsome clothes and many other fineries.(29) On one occasion the emperor, being in his bathing-room, called Leon and his sons before him, treated them most kindly, and was so pleased with the prowess of Rouben, that he made him one of his household, and promised to raise him yet higher.

Rouben once took the bathing tub of the emperor, which was full of water, and swung it quickly round, which excited much surprise. The news reached the emperor, and all who saw the act called him a new Sampson; but this excited envy in the soldiers and filled them with hatred. They gained the ear of the emperor, accused Rouben, and ultimately killed him by their wicked devices.(30)

Thoros was now left alone with his father in prison, where he had a dream, which he instantly imparted to his father. "I saw in a dream," said he, "a man of very superior appearance offering me a loaf of bread, on which was a fish; I being very astonished, took from the man what he offered to me; when thou, Oh father! earnest, and I enquired the meaning of that; but what further happened I know not." Leon, hearing these words from his son, was enlightened by heaven, and turning to him joyfully, embraced him ardently and said: "Be joyful, O my honourable son! for thou wilt be honoured as thy forefathers. After evil cometh a twofold good fortune,—our country, which was taken from us on account of our sins, and other lands, will again be governed by thee. The fish which thou hast seen, means,—that thou wilt be master of the sea, but I shall not enjoy these good tidings."

Leon died and was elevated to Christ; the emperor then felt compassion for Thoros, 1141 took him out of prison, and received him into the imperial guards. Being now in the imperial palace, and a soldier among the soldiers, he very soon distinguished himself, and even the emperor looked upon him with benevolence. Before the end of the year (1141) the emperor left Constantinople with a large army, and went to assist the Prince of Antioch, who was hard pressed by the Turks.(31) Being on a hunting party in the valley of Anazarbus, one of his own poisoned arrows wounded him, and he fell dead on the spot; he thus met with his deserved fate.(32) The army buried him on the place where he lost his life, and erected a monument which is even now to be seen, called *Kachzertik*, that is, *The corpse of the Calos, or Beautiful.*(33)

The Greek army returned, but Thoros remained in the country; though the traditions concerning this fact are different. Some say, Thoros withdrew himself quite alone, went by sea from Antioch to Cilicia, and took possession of his dominions, finding means to gain at first the town of Amouda, and afterwards all the other places. But the emperor's party say that Thoros, during the time the Greeks stayed in the country, lived with a lady who gave him a great sum of money; with these treasures he fled to the mountains, and discovered himself to a priest as the Son of Leon, the true king of the country. The priest was exceedingly happy at these tidings, and Thoros hid himself under a shepherd's disguise. 1143 There were many Armenians in this part of the country who, being barbarously treated by the Greeks, sighed for their former masters; to these men, as it is said, the priest imparted the joyful tidings; they instantly assembled and appointed *Thoros* their *Baron*;(34) he gained possession of Vahga, and afterwards of many other places. Let this be as it may, it was certainly ordained by God that this man, who was carried away as a prisoner, should become the chief of the country of his forefathers, that he should take the government out of the hands of the Greeks, and destroy their armies.

After the death of the Porphyrogenitus, his *son* Manuel succeeded him, who is commonly called *Pareser, the Virtuous.*(35) Immediately after he had taken possession of the empire, Manuel assembled an army to assist the Franks, who came by sea to these countries, and were hardly pressed by the Turks. Coming to Cilicia, and hearing what Thoros had done; how he wronged the Greeks, and behaved himself as the master of the country, the emperor became very angry, and ordered that Thoros should be brought to him a prisoner, which he thought an easy matter. But Thoros shut himself up in a steep and high fort, occupied all the narrow passes by his soldiers, and easily repulsed from thence the Greeks, many of whom were taken and brought in fetters before the victor. 1146 Manuel being informed of what had happened, became still more enraged.(36)

It happened that the emperor sent at that time, under the guard of many great men, a large sum of money, and that Thoros took the guard and the treasure, and divided the latter among his soldiers. These Greek nobles seeing this, said to Thoros: "Having taken such great riches, why dost thou squander them away to the common people?" Thoros answered nothing to this question, and only remarked: "These same men will bring you back to fetters, although you are now allowed to return to your friends."(37) The emperor heard with astonishment what these men, on their return, reported to him, and wished to keep on good terms with Thoros. The Prince of Antioch became the umpire between them. The emperor came to Antioch, where also Thoros was invited, and gained the admiration of every body by his prowess and valour. The emperor wanted Anazarbus and many other places, which were in the possession of Thoros; he accordingly delivered them up for a large sum of money.

Thoros returned to Cilicia, and the emperor put a stop to the campaign in order to return to his own country. As soon as the imperial army started from Anazarbus, Thoros proceeded suddenly in the night time to Vahga. Now, whether the king presumed upon(38) any thing, or whether some communication had been made to him, he did not wish to hold to the treaty. Thoros, as soon as the Emperor Manuel went back, again began his inroads. He again took Anazarbus and conquered Mamestia and the surrounding towns. The Duke of Tarsus, who was appointed governor of the country by the emperor, hearing of these proceedings of Thoros, assembled the great Greek army left him by the emperor, and those Armenian barons who belonged to the emperor's party, and enjoyed many honours by his kindness, such as Oscin the baron of Lampron, and the family of Nathaniel, who were the chiefs of Asgourhas.(39) They now united together to besiege Mamestia; when Thoros behaved himself very valiantly. With only a few men he made a sally out of the town, gained a complete victory over a large army, and took many prisoners; some of the Greeks he put to death, while others gained their liberty for a ransom. His Armenian captives he set instantly at liberty, and contrived to gain their friendship. Oscin having been won by a large sum of money, gave up his connexion with the emperor, and made a treaty with Thoros; and Thoros gave his daughter in marriage to the son of Oscin.(40) The Baron having thus settled his affairs collected a fresh army, took the famous Tarsus, and all the country from the precipices of Isauria(41) to the sea; he conquered Cilicia, beginning from Isauria, from one end to the other. The Emperor Manuel hearing these occurrences grew enraged on feeling himself unable to chastise Thoros. He sent a message to the Sultan of Iconium,(42) Chlish-Aslan, and promised him a great sum of money if he would make war against Thoros. The first time, the sultan objected to the treaty which existed between him and Baron Thoros, and so withstood the temptation; but his reluctance was overcome by a second message. 1154 He collected a large army, carried them into Cilicia, descended into the plain, and besieged Anazarbus. But God was against them and punished them with plagues, like those of the Egyptians; he sent flies and wasps against the infidels, and harassed them with many other heavy calamities. Thoros made inroads into the Sultan's own country, won Iconium itself, returned with a large booty, and sent Chlish-Aslan a present out of the booty. By this, and by the hardships they suffered, the Sultan and his followers were disgusted, and returned to their own country. 1156 They came back a second time, and returned again in confusion. The Sultan then kept his oath, and remained the friend of our hero.

Thoros was of a tall figure and of a strong mind: his compassion was universal; like the light of the sun he shone by his good works, and flourished by his faith; he was the shield of truth and the crown of righteousness; he was well versed in the Holy Scriptures and in the profane sciences. It is said that he was of such profound understanding, as to be able to explain the difficult expressions of the prophets—his explanations even still exist.(43) In a word, he was so accomplished in every thing, that God was pleased to call him to heaven. 1167 He was buried in Trassarg.

His brother Stephanus, of whom we have spoken before, remained near the *Black Mountain*, making himself illustrious by his prowess, and gaining Carmania and the surrounding places;(44) but the Greeks came again against him, and he was consumed by the "seething pot."(45) He died in the field and was buried in the church of Arkagal (or the Archangel). He left two sons, Rouben and Leon, who became afterwards king of Cilicia.

Thoros left a child under age, whom he committed, together with the country, to the care of a certain Baron and Baillie Thomas, his father-in-law, with an injunction to deliver to him the country as soon as the child should have attained his majority.(46) 1168 *Meleh*, of whom we have spoken above, was with the Sultan of Aleppo, and hearing of the death of his brother, he came with an army into the country, and dealt very cruelly with its inhabitants. Not being able to conquer the possessions of his brother he returned to Aleppo, and came back with still greater forces. Receiving a message from the Armenian Barons that they would freely acknowledge him as their sovereign, he sent back the Turks, and governed in peace for some time. But he soon drove into exile the Baillie Thomas, who went afterwards to Antioch. The child of Thoros was killed by the command of Meleh by some wicked people. 1169 This cruel man was at last killed by his own soldiers, and buried in the church called *the great Car.*(47)

The sons of Stephanus, Rouben and Leon, were very much honoured by a certain Baron *Pakouran*, by the whole Armenian nobility, and the army; they therefore appointed *Rouben* as their Baron. 1174 He was an excellent prince, compassionate and kind; he ruled the country very well, and was praised by every body. He was a friend of the Greeks, and married a lady of that nation, by whom he had two daughters blooming in chastity. He besieged Lampron and pressed its inhabitants very hard; they not being able to withstand him, called the Prince to their assistance; he 1182 invited Rouben to Antioch, and fraudulently held him a prisoner, thinking to conquer Cilicia with ease during his captivity. But his brother Leon and the army behaved themselves very valiantly; they pressed Lampron so closely in the absence of the Baron, and defended their own country so well, that they released Rouben and acknowledged his supremacy. The inhabitants of Lampron gave themselves and their treasure up to the Baron of Cilicia. On his return to his own country Rouben was kind and humane to every one, and at his death left the crown to Leon; he gave him many rules concerning the government of the country, and committed to him his daughters, with an injunction not to give them foreign husbands, that the Armenians might not be governed by foreigners and harassed by a tyrant. 1185 Rouben was buried in Trassarg.

*Leon* was a valiant and learned prince; he enlarged his principality and became the master of many provinces. A few days only after his taking possession of the country, the descendants of Ismael, under the command of one Roustam, advanced and came against Cilicia.(48) 1186 Leon was not frightened, but confiding in God, who destroyed Sanacherib, he vanquished with a few men the great army of the infidels. Roustam himself being killed by St. George,(49a) the whole Hagarenian army then fled and dispersed; the Armenians pursued them and enriched themselves by the booty. The power of Leon thus increased, and being confident in his strength, he chased the Tadjiks(49b) and pursued the Turks; he conquered Isauria and came as far as Iconium; he captured Heraclea,(50) and again gave it up for a large ransom; he blockaded Cæsarea,(51) and had nearly taken it; he made a treaty with the Sultan of Iconium, and received a large sum of money from him; he surrounded Cilicia on every side with forts and castles; he built a new church called Agner, and was exceedingly generous to all monasteries erected by his ancestors; his bounty extended itself even to the leprous; they being shunned by every body and expelled from every place, he assigned to them a particular house, and provided them with necessaries.

By such proceedings Leon attained a great name and became known to the Emperor of the Franks and the Greeks, and both, by Heavens' grace, favoured him with the diadem; and, indeed, the mission by which Leon the Great was crowned King,(52) was very famous. Jan. 6, 1198 The Armenians assembled together in the city of Tarsus, and in the cathedral of that town the Catholicos(53) anointed Leon, as it is the custom, king of the house of Thorgoma,(54) to sit on the throne and flourish in kindness; to glorify the church, and to govern well the country; to collect together the dispersed people, and to renovate its power; lastly, to fill the country with peace and to make it as happy as paradise.

This great king brought the Prince of Antioch over to him, by marrying to him his niece, the daughter of his brother. He then made an inroad into the province of Arasu and conquered the place called Balresay; by his excellent wisdom he also gained Lampron.

1201 The great Sultan of Iconium Caicaiuss(55) marched from Camir against the king, and besieged the fort Capan. The unruly Armenian troops attacked the enemy without waiting for an order of the king, and being partly killed and partly taken prisoners, the Turks pressed very hard the fort Capan. Leon did not let his spirits droop by this defeat; he collected what troops remained with him, and went plundering the territories of the Sultan as far as Camir. He laid waste the Sultan's country, and returned with a large booty. Hearing this the Sultan started from Cilicia to his own principality, and made peace with Leon, on the condition that the booty should be restored.

Leon, having governed the country twelve years as Baron and twenty-two as King, felt his end approaching, and appointed in an assembly of the whole nobility of the kingdom, a certain baron named Atan to be Regent(56) of the country and guardian of his daughter. Leon died soon after and was buried in the church of Agner; a part of his body was brought into the town of Sis, and a church was built thereupon.

May 1, 1219 After the assassination of Atan, Constantine was appointed regent, when he gave the daughter of the king and the heiress of the empire (the good and chaste lady Isabella), in marriage to one of the family of the king, the barons acknowledged him as their lawful sovereign, 1220 and swore the oath of allegiance.(57) But there arose a disturbance in the country; one Rouben(58) came from the Prince of Antioch, gained over many of the nobility and aspired to the crown. He soon took possession of Tarsus and was about to march against Sis; but Constantine met him near Tarsus with a great army, and vanquished this enemy. Rouben and the chief men of his party died in prison.

By this victory Constantine became more powerful, and governed the country with a firm hand; he built churches and honoured the clergy. At this time the patriarch was called John, the sixth since Nerses, from whom, as we have said, we began our chronicle, and think it therefore proper to mention these blessed persons.

After the death of Nerses, that is to say, after his migration from one life to another, Gregorius, called *Degha*, or the *child*, was anointed. He was a fine and strong man. After him Gregorius, called *Carawesh*, or *killed by the stone*;—then Gregorius Abirad;—and at last John, whom we have before mentioned.(59) Leon entered into a dispute with John, and appointed David in his place. This man governed the church for two years in an excellent manner: but after this, the king being reconciled to John, elevated him again on his seat. After this reconciliation king Leon fell sick and died, very much lamented by the Armenians. 1223 The Lord Constantine succeeded him, who excelling in kindness, betrothed the heiress of the empire, Isabella, before an assembly of the whole nobility, to his son Hethum.(60)

Hethum was then anointed king of Armenia; he was crowned with a golden crown, and held a golden consecrated sceptre in his hand, with a globe mounted in gold; he was placed on a high golden throne, and having these signs of royalty in his right hand, he promised to deal justice to the people at large and protect the poor from injustice. Hethum was an excellent and gracious king; fine and handsome in body and soul; religious, kind, compassionate, upright, bountiful, and generous. The lawful heiress of the empire, Isabella, governed the country together with her husband, and led a pious, religious life. She was blessed for her good deeds and exemplary life by many children, the numerous offsprings of a famous race.(61) The first was the pious Leon, who is now the anointed king, and after him Thoros, the blessed, who died the death of a hero.(62) Isabella brought also into the world five daughters and another son, Rouben, who died young. 1252 The queen being near the end of her life, and staying in a place called *Ked*, she heard a voice from heaven, crying aloud, "come my dove, come my love, thy end is near." She felt joyful on this happy vision, imparted it to the bystanders, and died in the Lord; her body was brought to the grave by a large assembly of the priesthood and laid in consecrated earth.

After the death of the Queen, the King was much occupied in the government of his country; for there arose an insolent people from the north, called *Tatars*, and also called, after their country, Mugal or Mogul,(63) who laid waste all the countries which fell into their hands. The words of the prophet Jeremiah, that "the seething pot will run over from the north," have been found true a second time, this being the case we must expect the same consequences. There were four kings, each of whom was accompanied(64) by ten chiefs, which is even now the case. These four kings met together with their ten followers; one arose and spoke with a loud voice in this high assembly, and he being foremost in power, was declared "*The son of God in heaven*."(65) 1254 To him went king Hethum,(66) and there remained four years. Hethum had considerable trouble, but he obtained friendly words, and a written treaty after the custom of the Tatars.(67) He then came back with great honours and conquered many provinces; he routed the armies of the Persians or Turks,(68) and took their country; he won by force Carmania; and Sebehesny was taken out of the hands of the Turks, whose splendour faded away.(69) God's will was changed, and he looked again on us with a benevolent eye; the doors of heaven were opened to let through his kindness on earth. The country was fruitful and happy like paradise, and every man sat in peace, as it is said in the scriptures, under his own vine. But the Armenians in Cilicia caused themselves, like in former times, Sodom and Ghomora, by their intemperance and wickedness to be very soon devoured by the wrathful fire(70) of heaven.

1265 The proud slaves who governed Egypt took by force Damascus, very hard pressed the Sultan of Berea or Aleppo, and conquered all the country called by the name of Shem.(71) These slaves united themselves with all the other Hagarenians, and it was as if the sand of the sea arose to grasp swords and daggers, and to fight the battles of men; they went against the Christians, like avengers sent from God. The sea-coast (from Gaza to Cilicia) suffered in particular; all the forts were destroyed. Antioch, the great Antioch, fell into their hands—they burned the houses, and the inhabitants were carried away into foreign countries.(72) Having taken possession of the before-mentioned territories, they went against Cilicia, sent to Hethum and demanded tribute of him.(73) The king collected his soldiery under the command of his sons, and hurried himself away to the Moguls for aid.(74) He had not yet returned, when the Hagarenians came into the country; the army fled, but the princes remained. Thoros was killed in battle, and Leon was carried away prisoner from his country. 1266 This unfortunate country was destroyed by fire, and the inhabitants were put to the sword; but the forts, having received private encouragement from Leon, could not be taken by the enemy, who retreated from them with shame. The famous church in Sis and the town itself was given up to the flames, but the inhabitants had time to fly.

Having done whatever they chose, the enemy returned to his own country in great triumph, and with a large booty. After their departure Hethum returned at the head of a Mogulian army into his own kingdom, and saw all the misfortunes which had befallen him during his absence; he wept bitterly, but he did not despair, and placed reliance on the mercy of God. His son, who had been carried away a prisoner, being endowed with a courageous nature, did not let his spirits droop or show any fear; on the contrary, he cheered the captives and consoled every man; for some he provided food, for others he paid their ransom and set them at liberty. The army presented Leon to the Sultan, who continued in his own country, and who, looking on Leon and hearing his wise speech, received him graciously, and spoke very kindly to him. With the permission of the Sultan, Leon went to Jerusalem to adore the holy cross, and to pray for the remission of his sins. He then went back to Egypt, into that prison where Joseph was in former times. The priests admonished him to think only of God; moreover, he constantly read the Scriptures and was always ways absorbed in prayer. Therefore God looked upon him with compassion, and turned the heart of the Sultan to pity.

Leon, when taken prisoner, was thirty years of age; remaining one year and ten months in Egypt, he made a treaty with the Sultan, which was ratified by King Hethum his father. This being done, Leon was set at liberty with great demonstrations of honour. The whole country rejoiced when Leon returned to his father: crowds of people ran to meet and see him; he embraced them all, and received them with heavenly kindness. The king went, on foot, to thank God that he had lived so long as to see his son Leon again, and 1268 in the presence of the highly-gifted patriarch Jacobus,(75) the follower of Constantine, he earnestly entreated Leon to take on him the government of the country, and to be anointed King of Cilicia; but Leon could not, by all his entreaties, be moved to accept this offer; and Hethum was compelled, therefore, to see his son only Baron of the Armenians, until he could enjoy the kingdom. The king happened to fall sick at this time and never recovered. There was consequently a great consternation in the country, and the people united together to give him the surname of *Makar.*(76) 1269 Having finished this mortal, and gained an immortal life, he was buried in Trassarg, and was celebrated in a poem. The Baron Leon was so afflicted by the death of his father, that he fell into a mortal sickness, and although all men supplicated him to be speedily crowned King of Cilicia, he would not do it instantly, but mourned three months. The neighbouring sovereigns, the Sultan of Egypt, the Khan, and other princes, sent missions of peace to him, entreating that he might be crowned King of Cilicia. Moved and encouraged by these messages, he called a great assembly of Armenians to Tarsus with the patriarch to anoint him, and to fulfil the duties of the church. Leon received the sceptre with the golden globe in his right hand,—and the Holy Ghost descended on him,—to be king on the house of Thorgoma; to govern and to defend the flock after the law of God.

Leon, sitting on the throne of his forefathers, was gracious to every body; he pardoned those who had offended him, and was in general exceedingly humane; he augmented the officers of the royal household, and held the clergy in high esteem. He provided for the poor ecclesiastics, and generally for all poor people; in what place soever he stayed, the indigent were provided for from the court. This being known, many people came from foreign parts, soldiers and others, and remained months although not invited; their expenses were payed by the court. Leon benefited the clergy even more than his forefathers, and gave to the Vartabeds their proper rank,(77) for he was a friend of learning;(78) every person who was elevated to the dignity of a Vartabed received a present from the king, and it was registered as an eternal remembrance. The army received higher pay than before, and the king was so kind to every body, so generous, so compassionate,(79) that all were delighted; and the whole nation of Armenians became, as it were, renovated. Satan, the author of all mischief, saw this, and he contrived to fight against the king; he tempted him by misfortunes like Job; he tried him by many wounds, but the king was found of more patience than even Job himself, for Job spoke of his temptations with his friends, and uttered curses as the misfortunes came one after the other.

1273 Leon soon gained information of the plots of the chieftains of his own family, but confiding in God, he took away only their castles, and granted them their lives; he left it to the Lord to reward them after their designs. 1274 Now the Sultan of Egypt, breaking the treaty he made with King Hethum, came against this country; he did not so much as give any notice of his design. United with the Arabs and the Turcomans, the Sultan, without any one being aware of it, made an inroad into Cilicia. These Turcomans were a long time since in this country as shepherds; they here kept their winter quarters, and knew therefore all the passes and defiles.(80) 1276 United with these people the Egyptians harassed the country more than had ever been the case before; they penetrated into the mountains, discovered the recesses of men and beasts, and destroyed numbers; many were also killed who had been found in the flat country. Only those who were in forts and castles escaped, all the rest were taken. The country was surrounded on all sides and given to the flames; the enemy took Tarsus, burnt the beautiful and celebrated church of St. Joseph, and plundered the town; having done all this mischief, they retired.

King Leon, full of courage, wished to try the chance of a battle, but the barons left him and he had only a few soldiers; seeing the desolation of the country, he was very sorrowful, but consoled every body and encouraged the people by presents. Whilst he was sustaining these trials without scarcely uttering a sigh, one of his sons, of tender age, died, and he himself fell into a sickness from which he could scarcely be saved. Whilst yet depressed by his sufferings he lost a daughter, but through all this he became not impatient, and uttered not an angry word; he placed his confidence in God, and suffered his trials with calmness. But there remained yet another trial for the country at large; the country was visited by a heavy plague, of which many poor people died, so that the land could not be cultivated, and there was in consequence a want of the necessaries of life. The king did not let his spirits droop, he animated everybody, and said in the words of Job, "The Lord gave, and the Lord hath taken away, blessed be the name of the Lord! Naked came we into the world, and naked do we leave it again." 1276 In these days the Lord began to look on us again with kindness from above, and the words of the prophet Hosea were fulfilled, "The shadow of death fled from us miserable men;" the Lord became reconciled to the harassed and desolated nation of Armenia. For the beginning of better days we were indebted to the people, who made war against the king. Having plundered our country, the Sultan withdrew his army, but Leon then came forward, vanquished all his opponents, took a great booty and returned joyful into his own kingdom.(81) The Sultan of Egypt hearing this, sent a message to Leon for peace and friendship. The news of these victories spread very far, so that the Khan(82) heard of it, sent armour and weapons, and admonished Leon to carry on the war.

The Turks, who reign in Camir (Iconium), wished at this time to make a treaty with the Moguls to hurt us; they spoke in consequence very badly of us, and induced the Khan by a sum of money to make a treaty with them.(83) The Turks spoke then more freely, and accused us publicly, but they were soon undeceived; for as soon as the union was dissolved, the Moguls came and destroyed them by the sword, sent presents to our king, and behaved in general very kindly to him. By this behavior the king gained courage, made an incursion into Turkestan,(84) took a large booty and returned into his own country with great joy. The neighbouring kings hearing this were much astonished, and longed to be at peace with us. Leon forgot all the mischief they had done, and accepted with a kind heart their offerings of friendship; for he was benevolent by nature, and rejoiced in kind dealings; misfortune could not depress him, and good fortune could not elevate him; he looked only on God and to govern his country well.

Leon had three sons: Hethum, the first born, learned in the Scripture and clever in every branch of science; the second is called Thoros, and the third Sempad. The spouse of the king, the Queen Ceran, is famous for her fidelity and benevolence. So is our king, who by God's decree is placed over the country; may the Lord yet grant him a long and a peaceful reign.(85)

Now to the end of my work I will subjoin some observations. It has been said before, that when the Tadjiks came into our country, they burned the house of God;—that they took the crosses, the Scriptures, and all other holy materials, into their abominable hands and cast them into the fire with infamous jokes; and that they put the priests to the sword, and tortured all Christians. When all these misfortunes befell the country, some of the inhabitants bore them patiently, though reluctantly; and others became furious and uttered impious words, for they were blind in spirit and weak in faith. "Can this be," said they, "can this be a true judgment, by which we are condemned? Are we the only sinners of all the inhabitants of the world, that we alone should be ruined? or are the Tadjiks the men of righteousness, by whose hands we are killed: those unbelievers, soiled by every wicked deed?" But from this reasoning it would follow, that those who fell under the hall by which Sampson buried himself, were not killed by reason of their own sins; that the Galileans, who were put to death by Pilate, fell not by reason of their own wickedness, but by the judgment of the Lord! All who are not penitent will suffer the same punishment, God chastens him whom he loves.(86) To rest his hopes on God, and to be patient in misfortune, is the best way to live in this world and in the next. May Leon, King of the Armenians, the writer and the reader of this, be judged worthy to enter into this eternal and immortal world. To the praise and honour of the three persons and one God, now and for ever, world without end.

---

# NOTES.

## Note (1), page 23.

This is the famous patriarch Nerses Clajensis in the twelfth century, one of the best writers of the Armenian nation. Galanus (I. 239) is full of praise of him. "Nerses Clajensis," says he, "orthodoxus patriarcha, quem Armenia universa, ut sanctum illius ecclesiæ patrem et doctorem agnoscit, ejusque commemorationem in Liturgia et Menelogiis celebrat. Fuit poeta sacer, et hac quidem facultate adeo insignis, ut celebrioribus, meo judicio, vel Græcis vel Latinis poetis in suo cœquandus sit idiomate." But both the praises and the censures of Galanus are to be received with great caution; he is blinded by his orthodoxy, and praises and blames the authors not according to their merit, but according to their faith. Nerses has written much and on very different subjects; his elegy on the capture of Edessa (1144) by the Turks, and his correspondence with the emperor Alexius and Manuel, are the most interesting works for us and for history. The elegy of Edessa has been printed several times and in many places: most recently (1826) in Paris, but without a French translation. The Archbishop Somal is not well-informed, when he says, (Quadro della storia letteraria di Armenia. Venezia 1829, p. 84), "fu accompagnata da una versione francese." The correspondence of Nerses has only, as far as I know, been once printed, viz. at St. Petersburgh, 1788, 1 vol. 4to. His short and uninteresting chronicle of the History of Armenia has been often printed, and for the last time in 1824 in Constantinople. The Archbishop Somal says, that this work was corrupted by the interpolations of the schismatical editor ("audacemente dall'editore falsificata e con riprovevole temerita sparsa di alcune aggiunte erronee contro il Concilio ecumenico di Calcedonia.") It is strange that the Armenians, who entertain the tenets of their national church, and are styled schismatical by the proselytes of the Roman Catholic Church, accuse the orthodox editors at Venice of the same falsifications; the Armenians in India wish therefore to print all their works, particularly the religious ones, at the press of the Bishop's College in Calcutta. (See Bishop Heber's Journals, iii. 435. 3d edition.)

## Note (2), page 23.

This is king Leon III, who reigned from 1269 to 1289, and of whom the chronicler speaks at the end of his work.

## Note (3), page 23.

I imagine Vahram never read Lucretius: that author gives the same reason for writing *De Rerum Natura* in verse.

**Note (4), page 24.**

Epist. ad Rom., chap. xiii. in the beginning.

**Note (5), page 24.**

The reader may recollect the old Byzantine pictures, painted on a gold ground; there is a large collection of these pictures at Schleisheim, near Munich.

**Note (6), page 25.**

I feel regret for poor Vahram, who here shows himself a heretic; for notwithstanding that it was forbidden to add any article to the creed of Nice, or rather Constantinople, the Latins added the celebrated *filioque*, that is to say, that the Holy Ghost proceeded from the Father *and the Son*, and condemned all others as heretics who upheld the old church, and would not acknowledge these innovations. Vahram, the Raboun, or doctor, shows himself to be such a heretic. He even wrote some dissertations on the trinity and the incarnation, at the command of his master king Leon III, but they were never printed. The Roman Catholic author of the "Quadro della letteratura di Armenia" (p. 115), says, that even in these works Vahram "si prova scrittore di poco sana dottrina intorno al dogma della processione dello Spirito-Santo."

**Note (7), page 25.**

This is the language of all divines, and of those philosophers who think *whatever is, is right.* If the sins of mankind have produced Mahomed, why has Spain alone out of the nations of Europe been depressed? Were these Visigoths greater sinners than their brethren in the south of France or the Franks themselves? It is not a speculative opinion, but the truth of history, that man is the architect of his own fortune, and that the world belongs to the mighty.

**Note (8), page 25.**

The Turks were known in Europe as early as the beginning of the sixth century of our era, but the western writers tell us nothing satisfactory, either as to the name or the origin of this large division of the human race. The Chinese, who were earlier acquainted with their *Thoo kiouei*, are also contradictory in their statements. They say, the Thoo kiouei are a particular tribe or class of the Hioung noo, called by different names, and that they are called Thoo kiouei because their town near the Altai, or gold mountain, had the form of a *helmet*, and a helmet is called Thoo kiouei, *yn y wei haou.* Matuanlin, in his great work, B. 343, initio, says this is the cause why this people is so called. It is fortunate for historical literature, that this accomplished Chinese scholar had no system in view in compiling his work:

he quotes on the same page other accounts on the origin of the name *Thoo kiouei* and different traditions of the original history of this nation. It has been remarked by Klaproth (Asia Polyglotta, 212) that Thoo kiouei (or a very similar word) means, indeed, in the Turkish language a *helmet*. If the Hiong noo are Turks they cannot certainly be either the Huns of Attila or Fins. Concerning the tribes of the Turks nothing is known with any certainty; tribes rise and decay in Tartary like the sand-hills in the desert: who can count them? The reader may find a lively and true picture of this rising and falling of the different Turkoman tribes in a novel, by Frazer, called *Memoirs of a Kusilbash*, printed 1828, in three volumes. The different denomination of the same people, Turks and Turkomans, is already used by William of Tyre, the celebrated historian of the Crusades; it may be said that they differ one from another, like, in former times, the Highlanders and Lowlanders in Scotland. While describing the difference between Turks and Turkomans, we may use the words of Dr. Robertson, mentioning the attempt of King James II. to civilize the Highlands and Isles. That great historian has the following words:—"The inhabitants of the low country began gradually to forget the use of arms, and to become attentive to the arts of peace. But the Highlanders, or the Turkomans, retaining their natural fierceness, averse from labour and inured to rapine, infested their more industrious neighbours by their continual incursions." (*History of Scotland*, ad a. 1602.) Some modern authors think it worth their while to take notice of a fault of a copyist (τοῦϱκοι for ἰυϱκαὶ), and find therefore the Turks as early as in Herodotus, Pomponius Mela, and Plinius; but this is not so unfair as to make Laura, the beautiful and chaste Laura, responsible for eleven children, upon the faith of a misinterpreted abbreviation, and the decision of a librarian. (Lord Byron's Notes on Childe Harold, Canto iv. stanza 30, lines 8 and 9.)

### Note (9), page 26.

*The kings* are the different Arabian chiefs who ruled independently of the Caliph of Bagdad; the *emperor* is the Emperor of Constantinople, or the Roman emperor, as Vahram says, with the other authors of these times. (See Gibbon, ch. 57.)

### Note (10), page 26.

"The captives of these Turks were compelled to promise a spiritual as well as temporal obedience; and instead of their collars and bracelets, an iron horseshoe, a badge of ignominy, was imposed on the infidels, who still adhered to the worship of their fathers." (Gibbon, l. c.)

### Note (11), page 26.

This is not quite true; the Caliph of Bagdad,—which new town our author calls in his poetical style by the ancient name of Babylon,—could not move from his capital without the consent of the descendents of Seljuk, but they never chose Babylon as the seat of their empire; they had no metropolis, but they preferred Nishapur. Abul Fazel (Ayeen Akbery II. 337) places Bagdad 33, and Babylon 32° 15´ latitude; their longitude is the same; 80° 55´ from the Canary Islands.

### Note (12), page 26.

The myriads of Turkish horse overspread a frontier of six hundred miles from Tauris to Arzearum, and the blood of one hundred and thirty thousand Christians was a grateful sacrifice to the Arabian prophet. (Gibbon l. c.)

### Note (13), page 26.

This is certainly the truth; the Armenians fled in their despair from the new Mahometan to the old Christian enemy. It can be only national vanity or folly, to assert or suppose that the Emperor Michael would give the province of Cappadocia for a country trampled on by the Seljuks, under whose irresistible power he felt himself. The Cappadocians remembering how they were dealt with in former time by the Armenians, and in particular by Tigranes, could not receive their new guests with much pleasure; and this is the principal reason of the great disaster which soon followed.

Διέθηκε δὲ φαύλως αὐτοὺς Τιγράνης ὁ Ἀρμένιος, ἡνίκα τὴν καππαδοκίαν κατέδραμεν ἅπαντας γὰρ ἀναςάτους ἐποίησεν εἰς τὴν Μεσοποταμίαν, &c. (Strabo xii. 2, vol. iii. 2d ed. Tauchn.) It is stated by the American missionaries, who have visited Cappadocia, that about 35,000 Armenians are still living in this province. "Cappadocia has 30,000 Greeks and 35,000 Armenians." (Mr. Gridley, in the Missionary Herald, vol. xxiv, printed at Boston, p. 111.) Cæsarea has, according to the same authority, from 60 to 80,000 inhabitants, and of these 2,000 are Greeks, and 8,000 Armenians. (Herald, 260.)

### Note (14), page 27.

The origin of this name of the people is not known. The Armenians call themselves after their fabulous progenitor Haig, and derive the name *Armen* from the son of Haig, Armenag; but I have not much confidence in these ancient traditions of Moses of Chorene. The Armenians are a strong instance that religion and civilization only give a particular character and value to a people, and preserve it from being lost in the course of time. Where are now the thirty different nations, which Herodotus found (Melpom. 88), between the bay of Margandius and the Triopian promontory? The Armenians are certainly a tribe of the ancient Assyrians; their language and history speak alike in favour of it. Nearly all the words of Assyrian origin which occur in the Scriptures and in Herodotus can be explained by the present Armenian language. Their traditions say, also, that Haig came from Babylon; and

Strabo's authority would at once settle the question, if he did not affirm too much. The Arabian and the Syriac language, and consequently the people, are radically different from the Armenian.

These are the passages of the geographer alluded to: Τὸ γὰρ τῶν Ἀρμενίων ἔθνος καὶ τὸ τῶν Σύρων καὶ τῶν Ἀράβων, πολλὴν ὁμοφυλίαν ἐμφαίνη κατά τε τὴν διάλεκτον ... καὶ οἱ Ἀσσύριοι, καὶ οἱ Ἀριανοὶ, καὶ οἱ Ἀρμένιοι παραπλησίως τως ἔχουσι, καὶ πρὸς τούτους καὶ πρὸς ἀλλήλους ... τοὺς ὑφ' ἡμῶν Σύρους καλουμένους, ὑπ' αὐτῶν τῶν Σύρον Ἀρμενίους καὶ Ἀραμμαίους καλεῖσθαι. (Strabo i. 2, vol. i. 65, ed. Tauchn.) But the Aramæns or Syrians are quite a different people from the Armenians, and Strabo is quite wrong when he thinks that both names are commonly used to designate one and the same nation. There is a fabulous story of a certain Er, the son of a certain *Armenios*, a Pamphylian by birth (Plato de Rep. x), but such stories are of no value in sober history.

### Note (15), page 27.

This story is told with more details by some contemporary chroniclers. Cakig reigned or rather had the *name* of a king from 1042-1079, and he is the last of the Bakratounian kings, a family which began its reign under the supremacy of the Arabs in the year 859 of our era. As regards the geography, the reader may compare the Mémoires sur l'Arménie, by Saint-Martin.

### Note (16), page 27.

Armenia remained from the time of the Parthians a feudal monarchy, and for this reason I use the expressions of the feudal governments in the middle ages.

### Note (17a), page 27.

Dionysius, in his description of the earth, says (v. 642) that the mountain is called Taurus: οὕνεκα ταυροφανές τε καὶ ὀξυκάρηνον ὁδεύει οὔρεσιν ἐκταδιόισι πολυσχεδὲς ἔνθα καὶ ἔνθα; perhaps more poetical than true. "The road lies over the highest ridges of the Taurus mountains, where, amidst the forests of pines, are several beautiful valleys and small plains; there appears, however, no trace of cultivation, though there is ample proof that these mountains were anciently well inhabited, as we meet with scarcely a rock remarkable for its form or position that is not pierced with ancient catacombs." (Col. Leake's Asia Minor in Walpole's Travels, i. 235.)

### Note (17b), page 28.

This is the proper name for the possessions of Rouben; the Armenians begin generally the line of the kings of Cilicia with the flight of Rouben in 1080.

### Note (18), page 28.

That is to say, as far as the gulph of Issus or Scanderum. Cilicia and the sea-shore was also in former times once in the possession of the kings of Armenia,—"the country on the other side of the Taurus," as the ancients used to say. Strabo says, from the Armenians (xiv. 5, vol. iii. 321. ed. Tauchn.) that they, τὴν ἐκτὸς τοῦ Ταύρου προσέλαβον μεχρὶ καὶ Φοινίκης. Plutarch says, that Tigranes "had colonized Mesopotamia with Greeks, whom he drew in great numbers out of Cilicia and Cappadocia."—(Plutarch in Lucullo.)

### Note (19), page 28.

Constantine sent many provisions to the Franks, when they were besieging Antioch. The Armenians were happy to get such powerful allies against their enemies, the Greeks. Alexius could not be very well pleased with the creation of an Armenian Margrave by the Latins, of whom he extorted "an oath of homage and fidelity, and a solemn promise that they would either restore, or hold the Asiatic conquests, as the humble and loyal vassals of the Roman empire"—(Gibbon, iv., 131. London, 1826, published by Jones.) The Armenians translate *Margrave* by *Asbed*, that is, Chief of the cavalry.

### Note (20), page 29.

It is not easy to see what connexion there is between the resurrection of a hen, or a duck, with the death of a king. What were the principles of divination of these wise men, of whom Vahram speaks?

### Note (21), page 29.

The name of this fort is written differently by different authors; I could not consult the great geographical works of Indjidjean.

### Note (22), page 30.

I think that *Trassarg* and *Trassag* is the same word; the names of places seem to be very corrupted in the Madras edition of Vahram's Chronicle. Chamchean says the king was buried in the monastery *Trassarg*, which is very probable; but how could he say Thoros left no son? In these monasteries the Armenian literature and sciences in general were very much studied in the course of the eleventh and twelfth centuries; some of the greatest Armenian authors flourished in the time of the Crusades. In their libraries were collections of the old classics, with many translations of the Greek authors; "e da quest' opere," says the Archbishop Somal, "attinsero gli scrittori del corrente secolo (the 12th), quello precisione d'idee, quella nobilita di concetti, quella purezza di stile, per cui si rendettero veramente gloriosi." Quadro 80. Foreigners are at a loss to find all these good qualities in the Armenian authors of the twelfth century.

## Note (23), page 30.

With what caution the secretary of Leon III. relates the treachery of Leon I. We see by this passage that Chamchean is in the wrong in saying that Thoros left no son. (Epitome of the great history of Armenia, printed in Armenian, at Venice in the year 1811, p. 300.)

## Note (24), page 30.

Is not Mamestia the ancient Hamaxia? "Εἶθ Ἀμαξία ἐπὶ βουνοῦ κατοικία τις," says Strabo, ὕφορμον ἔχουσα, ὅπου κατάγεται ἡ ναυπηγήσιμος ὕλη, (vol. iii. 221 ed. Tauchn.) It is certainly the Malmestra of the Latins and Byzantines. This town is called Mesuestra, Masifa, and by other names. (Wesseling Itner, p. 580. See a note of Gibbon at the end of the 52d chapter.) Tarsus is very well known as the principal town of Cilicia, as the native place of many celebrated men, as the stoic Chrysippus, and of the Apostle Paul. The following passage of Xenophon's Expedition of Cyrus illustrates very well the province and the whole history of the Armenian kingdom of Cilicia. "Thence they prepared to penetrate into Cilicia; the entrance was just broad enough for a chariot to pass, very steep, and inaccessible to an army, if there had been any opposition.... From thence they descended into a large and beautiful plain, well watered and full of all sorts of trees and vines; abounding in sesame, panic, millet, wheat and barley; and is surrounded with a strong and high ridge of hills from sea to sea. After he had left the mountains he advanced through the plain, and having made twenty-five parasangas in four days' march, arrived at Tarsus," etc. (See Spelman's notes to his translation of the Expedition of Cyrus.) Tarsus has now only, as it is said, 3,000 inhabitants.

## Note (25), page 30.

The Armenian phrase has this double signification, and Leon indeed carried on a war against the Seldjuks and the Count of Antioch, who sought to deprive him by treachery of all his possessions. Baldwin was not ashamed of doing any thing to enlarge his dominions. I know not why Vahram speaks not a word about these matters. (See Chamchean, l. c. p. 301.)

## Note (26), page 30.

The old fabulous hero of Armenia, spoken of by Moses of Khorene.

## Note (27), page 31.

Gibbon, iii. 341.

## Note (28), page 31.

Joscelin I., Count of Edessa. (See the Digression on the Family of Courtnay.—Gibbon, iv. 224.) Why does not Vahram, where he speaks of the four sons of Leon, name this Stephanus, who lived in Edessa with his uncle? It seems that there is a corruption in the text. Should the name of *Stephanus* be hidden under *Stephane, the crown* of Thoros, or which is more probable, is a line fallen out of our text? It would be necessary to compare some manuscripts to restore the original text. Thoros never received the kingly crown; he was only Baron of Cilicia: *Stephane* seems, therefore, nothing else than *Stephanus.*

### Note (29), page 32.

This agrees with all that we know about the character of Calo-Johanes. "Severe to himself, indulgent to others, chaste, frugal, abstemious, the philosophic Marcus would not have disdained the artless virtues of his successor, derived from his heart, and not borrowed from the schools."—(Gibbon.)

### Note (30), page 32.

I am not able to look into the Byzantine version of this fact. Calo-Johanes was not the man to be easily deceived, and to persecute innocent persons; we know, on the contrary, that he pardoned many people implicated in high treason. Calo-Johanes, as Camchean says (l. c. 304), suspected also Leon and his other son Thoros, and they were again sent to prison.

### Note (31), page 34.

Our author has here the word *Tadjik*, a name by which he and the other Armenian historians of the middle ages promiscuously call the native Persians, the Gasnevides and the other Turks. The origin and the proper meaning of this word will perhaps never be ascertained; it has something of the vagueness of the ancient denomination of *Scythia* and *Scythians.* It is certain that, in the works which go under the name of Zoroaster, and in the Desatir, the Arabs are called *Tazi*, and it is likewise certain that the language of this people, which is now called *Tadjik*, is pure Persian; the Bochars are, in their own country, called Tadjiks. How and why the ancient Persian name of the Arabs should be given to the Persians themselves it is impossible to conceive. Elphinstone (Account of the Kingdom of Câbul, London 1819, vol. i. 492) thinks that the Arabs and Persians were, in the course of time, blended together into one nation, and became the ancestors of the Tadjiks; but why should Armenians, Arabs, Turks and Afghauns, call those mestizes with a name of the Pehlvi language, which means originally an Arab? It seems rather that *Tazi* and *Tadjik* are two different words; *Tazi* is the Persian name for *Arab*, and *Tadjik* the name of a particular race of people, of whom the Persians are only a tribe. I do not know on what authority Meninski (see Klaproth's Asia, Polygl. 243) relies, but it is certain that the Chinese distinguish between the *Ta she* (Arabs) and the *Ta yue* (the Tadjiks), of whom, as they say, the Po she (Persians) are only a tribe. The Chinese had no communication with the Arabs before Mahomed, but they heard of them by their intercourse with the Sassanides, and call them, therefore by the Persian name Ta she (9685, 9247), but the *Po se* (8605, 9669) are only, as they say, a tribe like some other tribes, who formed particular kingdoms of the Ta yue (9685, 12490), or Tadjiks. They have received the name *Po sse* from their first king, *Po sse na*; but the Chinese had no direct communication with Persia before Kobad or Cabades, Kiu ho to (6063, 3984, 10260), as they spell the name, in their imperfect idiom, who became known to them by his flight and misfortunes. (See Matuanlin, l. c. Book 338, p. i, and following; Book 339, p. 6 a., p. 8 a., and the history of the *Ta she* or Arabs, p. 18, b. l. c.) But I am in doubt of Matuanlin, who makes the Masdeizans, followers of Buddha; he calls the Ateshgahs *Fo sse* (2539, 9659), Temples of Buddha, (l. c. p. 6, b. l. 5.) The popular pronunciation of *Ta yue* is, in many Chinese dialects, *Tai yuet.* I myself have often heard these characters so pronounced in Canton, and it was then as nearly as possible the ancient name of the Germans, *Teut*, the brethren of the Persians; the Chinese know also that the Ye ta (12001, 9700), *Getae*, *Gothi*, belong to the race of the Tayuet (Matuanlin, Book 338, p. 11), &c. But what sober historian would draw conclusions from a similarity of names? Perhaps a close inquiry may carry us to some leading facts, by which we may be able to connect the information of the east and the west. It would certainly be strange to begin the history of the Germans with the extracts taken out of the Han and Tang shoo. When I say the history of the Germans, I mean the history of those remains of the Teuts who remained in Asia, for Germany was certainly peopled long before the Chinese got any information of the Ta yue. These races became only known in China under the great dynasty of Han. A keen etymologist may, perhaps, find the modern Tadjiks in the ancient Daai or Daae; he may suppose that the Persians, like the Parthians, were only a branch of the Scythians or Tatars, and with confidence adduce a passage of Strabo, where it is said that the greater part of the Scythians are known by the name of Daai, Οἱ μὲν δὴ πλεἱους τῶν Σκυθῶν Δάαι προσαγορεὑονται. (Strabo, Geogr. xi. 8, vol. ii. 430, ed. Tauchn.) I will only add, that the same Strabo thinks, that the Daci (Δάκοι) may in former times have been called Daï (Δάοι), but he distinguishes them from the Daae (Δάαι). (Vol. ii. 36.)

**Note (32), page 34.**

Only the wounded pride of an Armenian could say this.

**Note (33), page 34.**

Have any of our modern travellers seen this monument? Claudian, the famous Latin poet, had composed in Greek the Antiquity of Tarsus,

Anazarbus, Berytus, Nice, &c. Abul Fazel (Ayeen Akbery, ii. 348) places Tarsus long. 68° 40′, lat. 36° 50′. (See Note 24.)

### Note (34), page 35.

The Armenians did so in imitation of the neighbouring Franks; they took many customs from the Crusaders, and corrupted their language by the introduction of many foreign words.

### Note (35), page 35.

Is this surname of Manuel found in the Byzantine writers?

### Note (36), page 36.

Vahram is in the wrong; Andronicus, not Manuel himself was at the head of the army. (Chamchean, 306; Gibbon, iii. 344.) Thoros was on such rocks, as Xenophon in the Anabasis, speaking of the rocks of Cilicia, calls πέτρας ἠλιβάτους, "rocks inaccessible to every thing but to the rays of the sun." Homer makes often use of this expression.

### Note (37), page 36.

This is a very obscure passage in the original. Vahram is no friend of details, and he is every moment in need of a rhyme for *eal*; who can wonder, therefore, that he is sometimes obscure? This passage is only clear, upon the supposition that Thoros divided the ransom among his soldiers. This is also stated by Chamchean.

See Note 28.

### Note (38), page 37.

I do not know why Vahram calls Thoros all on a sudden *Arkay*, "king;" how the royal secretary exerts himself to draw a veil over the treachery of Thoros!

### Note (39), page 38.

Oscin is the father of a celebrated author and priest, Nerses Lampronensis, so called from the town or fort Lampron; he was born 1153, and died 1198. In the concilium of Romcla 1179, Nerses spoke for the union with the Latin church, and the speech he made on this occasion is very much praised by the Armenians belonging to the Roman Catholic Church. This speech has been printed at Venice with an Italian translation, 1812. (Quadro 94.) Galanus, as the reader may easily imagine, speaks in very high terms of Nerses (i. 325): "Cujus egregia virtus," says he, "digna plane est, ut acterna laude illustretur, nomenque ad ultimas terrarum partes immortali fama pervehatur." For us his most interesting work is an elegy on the death of his parent, master, and friend, Nerses Shnorhaly; he gives a biography of this celebrated Catholicus, with many particulars of the history of the time. Nerses Shnorhaly was not only an author and a saint, but also a great statesman.

### Note (40), page 38.

In the whole course of history the Armenian nobles shew a great party feeling and much selfishness. They were never united for the independence of their country; if one part was on the side of the Persians or Turks, we shall certainly find another on the side of the Greeks or Franks; and the native Armenian kings had more to fear from their internal, than from their external enemies.

### Note (41), page 38.

The history of the foundation of the Armenian kingdom in Cilicia is very like the history of the rebellious Isaurians, "who disdained to be the subjects of Galienus." Thoros possessed a part of this savage country; and we may say of him, what Gibbon said of the Isaurians: "The most successful princes respected the strength of the mountains and the despair of the natives." (Gibbon, iii. 51.)

### Note (42), page 38.

Iconium is mentioned as a station by Xenophon and Strabo; Cyrus staid three days in "this last city of Phrygia." St. Paul found there many Jews and Gentiles; and it is said that even now, in its decayed state, Conia or Iconium has 30,000 inhabitants. This town is above 300 miles from Constantinople. (Gibbon, iv. 152.) The chronology of the Seljuks of Iconium may be seen in the *Histoire des Huns, par Deguignes*. Kuniyah قنفيا is laid down by Abul Fazel (Ayeen Akbery, ii. 359), long. 66. 30., and lat. 41. 40. A description of the modern Konia may be seen in Col. Leake's Asia Minor, l. c. 223.

### Note (43), page 40.

I find him not mentioned as an author in the "Quadro della storia letteraria di Armenia." It seems that his explanations of the prophets are now lost. If the reader will compare the elogy of Thoros with the facts in Vahram's own chronicle, he will easily find that adulation, and not truth, dictated it.

### Note (44), page 40.

*Seav* or *Sev-learn*, *Black-mountain* (Karadagh). Here was a famous monastery. *Carmania* is the place which formerly was called Laranda, and this name is still, as Col. Leake remarks, in common use among the Christians, and is even retained in the firmans of the Porte. Caraman derives its name from the first and greatest of its princes, who made himself master of Iconium, Cilicia, etc. (Col. Leake's Asia Minor, l. c. p. 232.)

### Note (45), page 40.

An allusion to Ierem, i. 13.

### Note (46), page 40.

It is known that the feudal laws and institutions have been introduced into the possessions of the Franks in Asia. *Baillis*, or *Baillie*, written *Bail* in the Armenian language, means a judge, and the word is commonly found in this signification in the chronicles and histories of the middle ages. The *Baillis* possessed powers somewhat similar to those of the ancient *Comites*. We see here and in other instances, that the Baillis are older than the end of the twelfth and the beginning of the thirteenth century. At this time they began in France. (Robertson, note 23, to his View of the State of Europe before the History of the reign of the Emperor Charles V.)

### Note (47), page 41.

It is very probable that the murderer Andronicus and Meleh were acquainted with each other; their history and their crimes are something similar.

### Note (48), page 43.

Roustam was a Sultan of Iconium. (See the Chronology of these Sultans in Deguigne's Histoire des Huns.)

### Note (49a), page 43.

In the times of the Crusades, wonders and witchcraft or enchantment were daily occurrences; the Christians imputed all their defeats to diabolical opposition, and their success to the assistance of the military saints, Tasso's celebrated poem gives a true picture of the spirit of the times.

### Note (49b), page 43.

Here the author uses again *Tadjik* as the name of a particular people: but accuracy, I fear, is not the virtue of Vahram; he calls the Turks of Iconium, the sons of Ismael or Hagar, *i.e.* Arabs.

### Note (50), page 43.

Our author says not in what province these towns lay. Chamchean, being able to consult other native historians, informs us that Leon nearly took Cæsarea in Palestine.—Heraclea was perhaps also the town of this name in Palestine; it was a small town near Laodicæa in the time of Strabo. Τῇ Λαοδικεία πλησιάζει πολίχνια, τὸ, τε Ποσείδιον καὶ Ἡράκλειον.—Strabo iii. 361, ed. Tauchn.

### Note (51), page 43.

The old Samaria, called Cæsarea by Herodes, ἥν Ἡρώδης Σεβαςὴν ἐπωνόμασεν, Strabo iii. 372. See the description of this famous place in Carl Ritler's Erdkunde ii. 393. Chamchean, 315. Abul Eazel (Ayeen Akbery, ii. 337.) places it long. 66. 30. lat. 32. 50.

### Note (52), page 44.

This memorable transaction is fully described in the great History of Armenia by Chamchean, and in the work of Galanus, vol. i. p. 346 and following. Many letters of Leon and the Catholicos exist now only in the Latin translations (Quadro l. c. 99.), or better have not been heard of by the Mechitarists at Venice. Frederic I., to whom Leon was very useful in the time of the second crusade, promised the Baron of Cilicia to restore in his person the ancient kingdom of Armenia. After the unfortunate death of the emperor, Leon sent ambassadors to the Pope Celestinus III. and Henricus VI., to gratify his wishes; the ambassadors came back to Cilicia in the society of the archbishop Conrad of Mentz, bringing the crown from the emperor and the benediction of the pope. The Emperor of Constantinople, Alexius, sent also a crown to Leon "the Great." The king of Cilicia is, as far as I know, the only king who received the crown by both the emperors of the west and the east, and by the consent of the pope. The pope hoped to bring the Armenians under his sway, and the Latins and the Greeks thought Leon a very useful ally against the overpowering Saladin.—See the Letters in the Appendix.

### Note (53), page 44.

*Catholicos of Armenia* is the title of the Armenian patriarch. Gregorius VI., called Abirad, was Catholicos at this time; he was elected in the year 1195, and died 1203. The Latins had a very high opinion of the power of an Armenian patriarch. Wilhelm of Tyrus, speaking (De Bello Sacro, xvi. 18.) of the synod of Jerusalem in the year 1141, has the following words: "Cui synodo interfuit maximus Armeniorum pontifex, immo omnium episcoporum Cappadociæ, Mediæ et Persidis et utriusque Armeniæ princips et doctor eximius qui *Catholicus* dicitur." Wilhelm might add, "et Indiæ," for I think that the Armenians, like the Syrians, formed as early as the sixth century of our era, settlements in this part of the world. It is certain that Armenians were in India as early as the year 800. (*De Faria*, in the *Collection of Voyages and Travels*, by Kerr, Edinburgh 1812, vol. vi. p. 419.)

### Note (54), page 44.

The Armenians consider themselves the descendants of *Thorgoma* (a name differently spelt in the different manuscripts and translations of Genesis x. 3.) the son of Japet.

### Note (55), page 44.

Vahram is too concise; he never gives the reasons of occurrences. I see, in Chamchean, that Leon married, after the death of his first wife, a daughter of Guido, king of Cyprus, by whom he had a daughter, called Sabel or Elizabeth, his only child and heiress of the kingdom. The Sultan of Ionium did not like these intimate connexions of the Armenians with the Latins; he feared some coalition against himself, and he thought it proper to be beforehand with the enemy.

### Note (56), page 45.

We have in the text again *Bail* or *Bailly*. I could not translate the word otherwise than *Regent*: this is certainly the sense in which Vahram uses this expression.

### Note (57), page 46.

The name of this first husband of Isabella was Philippus, the son of the Prince of Antioch and the niece of Leon. Philippus died very soon, and Isabella, as our author says himself, married, 1223, the son of the regent Constantine, Hethum or Haithon.

### Note (58), page 46.

This Rouben was of the royal family.—Chamchean, 326.

### Note (59), page 46.

It would carry us too far if we were to attempt to elucidate the ecclesiastical history of these times, for there were many synods and many negotiations between the Armenian clergy and the Greek and Latin church, concerning the union. Pope Innocent III. showed also at this opportunity his well-known activity. There exist many letters from the Catholici and the Armenian kings to different popes and emperors, with their answers,—ample matter for a diligent historian. The first Gregorius after Nerses is Gregorius IV. from 1173-1193. Gregorius V. from 1193-1195. Gregorius VI. from 1195-1202. John VII. from 1202-1203. David III. from 1203-1205, and then again John VII. 1205-1220. Constantine I. from 1220-1268. There were yet two anti-Catholici, elected by a dissentient party, who are not mentioned by Vahram.

### Note (60), page 47.

The good Vahram seems to have forgotten what he said a short time before. I do not know by what genealogy Chamchean could be induced to say that Hethum is an offspring of Haig and the Parthian kings.

## Note (61), page 48.

The flattery of Vahram increases as he comes nearer to his own time. I have sometimes taken the liberty to contract a little these eulogies; the reader will certainly be thankful for it.

## Note (62), page 48.

In the battle against the Mameluks of Egypt in the year 1266.

## Note (63), page 48.

The Moguls are a branch, a tribe, or a clan of the Tatars; so say all well-informed contemporary historians and chroniclers; so say in particular the Chinese, who are the only sources for the early history of the Turks, the Moguls, and Tunguses; nations which, in general, from ignorance or levity, have been called *Tatars*—the Moguls only are Tatars. The Armenians write the name *Muchal*; in our text of Vahram, *Muchan* has been printed by mistake. That this people was called so from their country is quite new; and if this were the case, it would be still a question why the territory was called *Mogul*. There are sometimes such whimsical reasons for the names of places and nations, as to defy the strictest research and the greatest curiosity. The name of *Mogul* seems not to be older than Tshinggis, and Mr. Schmidt in St Petersburgh, derives the word from a Mongolian word, which means *keen, daring, valiant*. The ancient name of the Moguls, as it is given by the native historian Sätzan, is, I am afraid, only a mistake of this ignorant chieftain. His whole history of the Moguls is only a very inaccurate compilation from Chinese authors, and the unlettered Mogul may have taken the appellative expression pih teih 8539, 10162, or pih too 10313, 8539, "northern barbarians" or "northern country," for the proper name of his forefathers. Long before the Moguls, the Chinese became acquainted with some barbarous tribes called by different names, and also *Mo ho*; but the Chinese authors, who are so accurate in giving the different names of one and the same people, never say that the *Mung koo*, who are also written with quite different characters, are called *Mo ho*, or *vice versâ*. These Mo ho are described as quite a distinct people, with a particular language, divided into different clans or kingdoms. There is an interesting description of this people under the name of Wŭh keih 14803, 5918, in the Encyclopædia of Matuanlin, Book 326, p. 146. The same author says, in the sequel of his great work, that the Kitans have nearly the same customs (sŭh 9545) as the Mo ho, but he does not say that they are of the same race of people.—Matuanlin, Book 345, in the beginning. The different names of the Mo ho are also collected in Kanghi's Dictionary under hŏ, a character not to be found in Morrison's Tonical Dictionary; it is composed out of the rad. 177, and the sound giving group hŏ, 4019, and there also exists no passage saying Mo ho and Mung koo are one and the same people.

### Note (64), page 49.

Vahram speaks of the four sons of Tshinggis. The army of the Moguls and of Timur (see his Institutes, p. 229 foll.) was divided into divisions of 10, 100, 1000, &c. The ten followers were the ten first officers or "Comites," as Tacitus calls the compeers of the German princes. Similar customs are always found in a similar state of society.

### Note (65), page 49.

Vahram confounds probably the first election of the Emperor Cublai, with the election of his follower Mangou, to whose residence at Caracorum the King of Cilicia, Hethum, went as a petitioner. Vahram knows that the title of the head of the Mongolian confederacy is Teen tze, 10095, 11233, "the son of Heaven." The Mongolian emperors have only been called so, after the conquest of China by Cublai. *Teen tse* is the common title of the Emperor of the "Flowery empire." According to other accounts, Tshinggis called himself already "Son of Heaven."

### Note (66), page 49.

To Mangou khan; we know this by other contemporary historians. There exist some Armenian historians in the 13th century, who contain a good deal of information regarding the Moguls. One is printed in the Mémoires sur l'Arménie, by Saint-Martin. See Quadro della Storia, &c. p. 112, and following.

### Note (67), page 49.

Is this treaty to be any where found? It would certainly be very interesting. Vahram has the word *kir*, by which it is certain that Hethum I. returned with a written treaty, which very probably was written in the Mogulian language, and with the Mogulian characters.

### Note (68), page 49.

Vahram has again the unsettled and vague name of Tadjik.

### Note (69), page 49.

Vahram died before the beginning of the glory of Othman, and of the increasing power of his descendants; he speaks of the fading state of the Seljuks of Iconium.

### Note (70), page 50.

I have taken the liberty to shorten a little the pious meditations of our author; he would have done better to give us some details regarding the interesting transactions with the Moguls.

## Note (71), page 50.

Sem, the son of Noe,—our author means Palestine and Syria. The Mamalukes of Egypt remained in possession of Sham, or Syria, till the conquest of Timur, 1400 of our era. He mentions in his Institutes, p. 148, the Defeat of the Badishah of Miser and Sham شام After the retreat of Timur, the Mamalukes again took possession of the country, and held it till the conquest of the Othomans. "Egypt was lost," says Gibbon, "had she been defended only by her feeble offspring; but the Mamalukes had breathed in their infancy the keenness of the Scythian air; equal in valour, superior in discipline, they met the Moguls in many a well-fought field, and drove back the stream of hostility to the eastward of the Euphrates."—Gibbon iv. 270. See also p. 175, 261. It is known that "this government of the slaves" lasted by treaty under the descendents of Selim, and was only destroyed in our times by a signal act of treachery of Mehmed, Pasha of Egypt.

## Note (72), page 50.

"Antioch was finally occupied and ruined by Bondocdar, or Bibars, Sultan of Egypt and Syria."—Gibbon iv. 175. Antioch never rose again after this destruction; it is now in a very decayed state, and has only about 10,000 inhabitants. The Turks pronounce the name *Antakie*.

## Note (73), page 50.

Confiding in his Mogulian allies, or masters, Hethum took many places, which formerly paid tribute to the Mamaluke sovereigns; they asked of him, therefore, either to restore them their former possessions, or to pay tribute.—Chamchean, 339.

## Note (74), page 50.

This is certainly very remarkable. It had never happened before in the history of the world, and will perhaps, never happen in future times, that the kings of Georgia and Armenia, the Sultans of Iconium, the Emirs of Persia, the ambassadors of France, of Russia, of Thibet, Pegu, and Tonquin, met together in a place about nine thousand miles to the north-west of Pekin, and that life and death of the most part of these nations depended on the frown or smile of a great khan. M. Rémusat has written a very learned and ingenious dissertation on the situation of Caracorum.—Abul Fazel (Ayeen Akbery ii. 336, London edition, 1800), lays down قراقوروم Caracurem, long. 111. 0. lat. 44. 45. All the residences of the khan were distinguished by the general name of *Kharibaligh* (town or residence of the khan), and this has led astray many historians and geographers.

## Note (75), page 52.

Jacobus I. died 1268, and is considered a very great man by the Armenians; they call him the *Sage* and the Doctor. Jacobus has written some ecclesiastical tracts, and a very fine song on the nativity of the Virgin Mary, which is printed in the Psalm-book of the Armenian church.

## Note (76), page 53.

This seems to be the Greek word μακαριος, "beatus," "blessed," &c.

## Note (77), page 54.

Nobody receives the degree of a Vartabed without having previously undergone a strict examination: it is something like the doctor of philosophy of the German universities; but a Vartabed, that is to say *a teacher*, is rather more esteemed in Armenia than a doctor of philosophy in Germany. The Vartabed receives at his inauguration a staff, denoting the power to teach, reprove, and exhort in every place with all authority. (See the Biography of Gregory *Wartabed*, as the word is spelt there, in the Missionary Herald, vol. xxiv. 140.) It is very probable that this institution came in the fifth century of our era from the philosophic schools in Athens to Armenia; nearly all the classical writers of this age went to Athens for their improvement.

## Note (78), page 54.

Leon III. gave orders to make new copies of all the works of the former classical writers of the nation; in our eyes, his greatest praise.

## Note (79), page 55.

The King's secretary cannot find words enough to praise his master; in his zeal, he accumulates words upon words which signify the same: I have passed over some of these repetitions. Vahram, without being aware of it, describes his master more as a pious monk than as a prudent king. Why does the Secretary of State not give any reason for the rebellious designs of the Armenian chieftains?

## Note (80), page 55.

From the time of Herodotus and Zoroaster to this day, the Turcomans carried on their nomadical life, and as it seems, without much change in their manners and customs. The text of Herodotus and Polybius may be explained by the embassies of Muravie and Meyendorn to Khiva and Buchara. Many of these Turcoman shepherds were driven to Asia Minor by the destruction of the Charizmian empire by the Moguls; the inroads and devastations of the Charizmian shepherds have been described by many contemporary authors, and the Crusaders experienced a great defeat from these savages.

### Note (81), page 57.

The Egyptians having retired, Leon went against their allies one by one.

### Note (82), page 58.

The successor of Hulagou, khan of Persia.

### Note (83), page 58.

Here Vahram calls even the Moguls Tadjiks,—is it because they governed Persia?

### Note (84), page 58.

Vahram calls here the territory of the Seljuks of Iconium *Turkestan.* As regards the etymology of the word, he is quite in the right; but what we are accustomed to call *Turkestan*, is a country rather more to the north-east.

### Note (85), page 59.

Here ends the Chronicle; but Vahram adds some reflections which I thought proper to subjoin, and only to pass over his so often repeated pious sentiments.

### Note (86), page 60.

The monk Vahram is not tired of repeating the same thought in twenty different ways, but I was tired of translating these repeated variations of the same theme, and the reader would probably have been tired in reading them. Why should we waste our time in translating and reading sermons, from which nothing else could be learned, than that the author said what had been said long before him, in a better style. Why should we think it worth our while to study the groundless reasoning of a mind clouded by superstition?

# APPENDIX.

## *Letters between Pope Innocent III. and Leon the First Armenian King of Cilicia.*

During the middle ages, the clergy governed the world, and the Pope, as the head of the clergy, was also the head of what then was called the Christian Republic. All transactions of any note are therefore contained, or at least spoken of, in the vast collections of letters or Regesta of the followers of St. Peter. To be united with the Roman Catholic Church was, in fact, (particularly during the Crusades,) the same as acknowledging the Pope as the supreme umpire, not only in the spiritual but also in the civil government of the country; this is clearly to be seen in the following letters. If the Popes could not speak to every king as they did to the impotent sovereign of Cilicia, it was certainly not their fault. The following letters exist only, as far as I know, in the Latin tongue, and are taken from the *Regesta Innoc. III.*, lib. ii., pp. 208, 209, 247, 44. I give the text of these letters according to Galanus, who accompanied them with a translation into the Armenian language. (Conciliat. Eccles. Arm. cum Romana. Romæ, 1650; vol. i., p. 357).

---

Leo Armeniæ Rex, Reverendissimo in Christo Patri et Domino, Innocentio, Dei gratia Summo Pont. et universali Papæ, tanto, ac tali honore Dignissimo.

*De suo erga veram Religionem, et Sedem Apostolicam amore; et quod petat auxilium contra Sarracenos.*

Leo per eandem, et Romani Imperii gratiam Rex omnium Armeniorum, cum salutatione seipsum, et quicquid potest. Gloria, laus, et honor omnipotent Deo, qui Vos tantum, et talem pastorem Ecclesiæ suæ præesse voluit, vestris bonis meritis exigentibus: et tam fructuosam, et firmam fabricam super fundamentum Apostolorum componere, et tantum lumen, super candelabrum positum, toti Orbi terrarum ad salutem totius Christianitatis effundere dignatus est. In vestri vero luminis gratia, salutaribus monitis Reverendiss. Patris nostri Archiepiscopi Moguntini,[4] instruct et informati *omne Regnum nobis à Deo commissum, amplissimum, et spatiosum, et omnes Armenios, huc illuc in remotis partibus diffusos, ad unitatem Sanctæ Romanæ Ecclesiæ*, divina inspirante dementia, *revocare cupimus, et exoptamus.* Ad hæc calamitates, miserias, paupertates, et imbecillitatem. Regni Syriæ,[5] et nostrum, per ipsum prædictum Moguntinum (quia difficilior labor erat scripto retexere) Pietati vestræ patefacimus. Ipse vero per singula rei veritatem vobis explicabit: in cujus notitiam ista non præteriere. Hanc utique contritionem, et collisionem in valle destituti lacrymarum jamdiu sustinuimus; quod de cætero sine spe subsidii, et auxilii vestri sustinere nequimus. Verum quia zelus domus Dei tepescere non debet in cordibus tam vestro, quam nostro, non ut personam instruentis geramus, ejusdem domus decorem diligere, et pro eadem domo murum nos oportet opponere; ut impetus, quem super eam faciunt inimici Crucis, co-operante Dei gratia, collectis in unum animi viribus, resistendo excludamus. Hinc est, quod vestram flexis genibus imploramus pietatem, quatenus lacrymabilibus Domini Moguntini precibus, et nostris divino intuitu aures misericordiæ porrigatis: et miseriis Christianitatis compatientes, subsidium Christianissimum nobis accurrendo mittatis, antequam irremeabile, quod absit, incurramus diluvium; immo cum Dei, et vestro auxilio, evaginato ense, de Hur Chaldæorum, et persecutione Pharaonis liberari possimus. Datum Tarsi, anno ab incarnatione Domini, MCXCIX. mense Majo. die xxiij.

---

*Innocentii III. ad præcedentem Leonis epist. responsio; qua laudat illius studium erga Sedem Apost. cujus primatum demonstrat; hortatur, ut in obedientia ejusdem S. Sedis fideliter perseveret; et subsidium contra Sarracenos cito se missurum pollicetur.*

Is Ecclesiam suam, congregatam ex gentibus, non habentem maculam, neque rugam super gentes et Regna constituit; is extendit palmites ejus usque ad mare, et usque ad terminos terræ ipsius propagines dilatavit; cujus est terra, et plenitudo ejus, Orbis terrarum, et universi qui habitant in eo, ipse etiam Romanam Ecclesiam non solum universis fidelibus prætulit, sed supra cæteras Ecclesias exaltavit: ut cæteræ ab ea non tam vivendi normam, et morum sumerent disciplinam, sed et fidei etiam catholicæ documenta reciperent, et ejus servarent humiliter instituta. In Petro enim Apostolorum Principe, cui excellentius aliis Dominus ligandi et solvendi contulit potestatem, dicens ad eum: quodcunque ligaveris super terram, erit ligatum et in cœlis: et quodcunque solveris super terram, erit solutum et in cœlis: Ecclesia Romana, sedes ejus, et Sessores ipsius Romani Pontifices, successores Petri, et vicarii Jesu Christi, sibi invicem per successivas varietates temporum singulariter succedentes, super Ecclesiis omnibus, et cunctis Ecclesiarum Prelatis, immo etiam fidelibus universis a Domino primatum et magisterium acceperunt: vocatis sic cæteris in partem solicitudinis, ut apud eos plenitudo resideat potestatis. Non enim in Petro, et cum Petro singulare illud privilegium expiravit, quod successoribus ejus futuris usque in finem Mundi Dominus in ipso concessit; sed præter vitæ sanctitatem, et miraculorum virtutes, par est in omnibus jurisdictio successorum; quos etsi diversis temporibus, eidem tamen Sedi, et eadem auctoritate Dominus voluit præsidere. Gaudemus autem, quod tu, sicut Princeps catholicus, Apostolicæ Sedis privilegium recognoscens, venerabilem fratrem nostrum Moguntinum Archiepiscopum, Episcopum Sabinensem, unum ex septem Episcopis, qui nobis in Ecclesia Romana collaterales existunt, benigne, ac hilariter recepisti; et non solum per eum institutis salutaribus es instructus, quibus juxta continentiam litterarum tuarum totum Regnum tuum licet amplissimum desideras informari, et universos Armenos ad Ecclesiæ Romanæ gremium revocare; sed *ad honorem, et gloriam Apostolicæ Sedis, quam constitutam esse novisti super gentes, et regna, diadema regni recepisti de manibus ejus*; et eum curasti devote, ac humiliter honorare: et nos per ipsum, et litteras tuas ad orientalis terræ subsidium invitasti. Ei ergo, a quo est omne datum optimum, et omne donum, perfectum, qui habet corda Principum in manu sua, quas possumus, gratias referentes, quod tibi tantæ humilitatis animum inspiravit; rogamus Serenitatem Regiam, et exhortamur in Domino, ac *per Apostolica tibi scripta mandamus*, quatenus in timore Domini, et Apostolicæ Sedis devotione persistens, ad expugnandam barbariem Paganorum, et vindicandam injuriam Crucifixi, tanto potentius, et efficacius studeas imminere; quanto fraudes et versutias hostium vicinius positus melius cognovisti: non in exercitus multitudine, aut virtute, sed de ipsius potius miseratione confidens, qui docet manus ad prælium, et digitos movet ad bellum; qu arcus fortium superat, et robore accingit infirmos. Jam enim per Dei gratiam ad commonitionem nostram multi Crucis signaculum receperunt, et plures Domino dante recipient, in defensionem orientalis Provinciæ opportuno tempore transituri. Jam etiam duo ex fratribus nostris de manibus nostris vivificæ Crucis assumpsere vexillum, exercitum Domini præcessuri. Confide igitur, et esto robustus, quia citius forsitan, quam credatur, orientalis Provincia subsidium sentiet expectatum. Dat. Later. viii. kal. Decembris.

---

*Idem Innocentius Papa ad illustriss. Regem Armeniæ. Quod ipsi transmittat vexillum beati Petri, quo contra Crucis inimicos utatur.*

*After some previous passages*:—Et tibi congaudemus, et Nobis, immo etiam universo Populo Christiano; quod eum tibi Dominus inspiravit affectum, ut Apostolicæ Sedis instituta devote reciperes, et præcepta fideliter observares, et contra inimicos Crucis propositum illud assumeres, ut in eos vindicare cupias injuriam Crucifixi, et hæreditatem ejus de ipsorum manibus liberare. Nos igitur de tuæ devotionis sinceritate confisi, ad petitionem dilecti filii Roberti de Margat militis, nuncii tui, in nostræ dilectionis indicium, vexillum beati Petri tuæ Serenitati dirigimus; quo in hostes Crucis duntaxat utaris, et eorum studeas contumaciam cum Dei auxilio, suffragantibus Apostolorum Principis meritis, refrænare. Datum Later. xvi. kal. Januarii.

---

*Leonis Armeniæ Regis ad Innocentium III. epistola; qua ad præcedentem respondet, et privilegium ab eo petit.*

*After some other passages*:—Paternitatis vestræ litteras, quas per dilectum fidelem Nuncium nostrum nobis direxistis, ea qua decuit reverentia, et devotione suscepimus; et per earum significata pleno collegimus intellectu, Vos charitatis visceribus Regiam Majestatem nostram amplexari. Continebant etiam quod in devotione, et amore Apostolicæ Sedis persisteremus; et in hoc semper perseverare cupimus; et optamus, et testis est rerum effectus, dum *de omnibus negotiis nostris ad Sedem Apostolicum appellamus*. Misistis autem nobis per eundem Nuncium vexillum sancti Petri in memoriale dilectionis Sedis Apostolicæ, quod semper ante nos portari contra inimicos Crucis ad honorem Sanctæ Romanæ Ecclesiæ faciemus ... Præterea nos obedientiæ vinculis de cætero Apostolicæ Sedi esse alligatos, non dubitetis; ea propter, si placet Sanctitati vestræ, cuilibet alteri Ecclesiæ Latinæ nec volumus, nec debemus alligari. Hinc est, quod Sanctitatem vestram humiliter flagitamus, quatenus nobis litteras apertas mittere dignemini, ut non teneamur videlicet cum Latinis de terra nostra de qualibet conditione, excepta sancta Romana Ecclesia, cuilibet Ecclesiæ Latinæ: et quod non habeat potestatem, nos, seu Latinos de terra nostra excommunicandi, vel sententiam in Regno nostro proferendi super Latinos quælibet Ecclesia, excepta, ut dictum est, Sede Apostolica.[6] Præsentium quoque latorem, dilectum, et fidelem nostrum militem, nomine Garnere Teuto ad pedes Sanctitatis vestræ dirigimus; cui super his, quæ ex parte nostra vobis indixerit, tanquam Nobis ipsis credere, ne dubitetis, &c.

---

*Ex indulto Regis Armeniæ, a Domino Papa Innocentio III. sibi facto.*

Volentes igitur, quantum cum Deo possumus, tuæ Serenitati deferre, et *cum honestate nostra petitineso Regias exaudire*; tuis precibus inclinati, auctoritate præsentium inhibemus, ne quis in te, vel Regnum tuum, aut homines Regni tui, cujuscunque conditionis existant qui mediantibus tamen ejusdem Regni Prælatis, Sedi Apostolicæ sunt subjecti, præter Romanum Pontificem, et ejus Legarum, vel de ipsius speciali mandato, districtionem Ecclesiasticam audeat exercere,[7] &c.

---

# CHRONOLOGY
## OF THE
## ARMENIAN BARONS AND KINGS OF CILICIA
## (ACCORDING TO CHAMCHEAN.)

| | |
|---|---|
| Rouben I. | 1080 |
| Constantine I. | 1095 |
| Thoros I. | 1100 |
| Leon I. | 1123 |
| *Interregnum* | 1138 |
| Thoros II. | 1144 |
| Thomas Bail, regent | 1168 |
| Meleh | 1169 |
| Rouben II. | 1174 |
| Leon II.[8] | 1185 |
| Sabel or Isabella, queen | 1219 |
| Philippus | 1220 |
| *Interregnum* | 1222 |
| Hethum or Haithon I. | 1224 |
| Leon III. | 1269 |
| Hethum II., also called Johannes | 1289 |
| Thoros III. | 1293 |
| Hethum II. (second time) | 1295 |
| Sembad | 1296 |
| Constantine II. | 1298 |
| Hethum III. | 1300 |
| Leon IV. | 1305 |
| Odshin | 1308 |

| | |
|---|---|
| Leon V. | 1320 |
| Constantine III. | 1342 |
| Guido | 1343 |
| Constantine IV. | 1345 |
| *Interregnum* | 1363 |
| Leon VI. | 1368 |
| End of the Armenian kingdom in Cilicia | 1375 |

---

# FOOTNOTES

[1] Nicetas II. p. 148. I wonder that Montesquieu, in making use of this passage of Nicetas (Grandeur et Decadence des Romains, ch. xxii.), has not been struck with its incorrectness; it did not escape the critical discernment of Gibbon: the Decline and Fall, etc. ch. 49. n. 17.

[2] Bruce's Annals of the East-India Company, iii. 88. The mercantile companies trading to different parts of Asia found every where the Armenians in their way; the Armenians became jealous on the new intruders of their commerce, and tried to remove them by intrigues. See Hanway, i. 303.

[3] Pompey the Great had vanquished the Albanians, who brought into the field twelve thousand horse and sixty thousand foot. Plutarch in Pompeio., t. ii. p. 1165. Gibbon, chap. xlvi. n. 6.

[4] See the Notes 53 and 54 to the text of Vahram's Chronicle.

[5] This part of Palestine and Syria, which belonged to the Latins.

[6] Leon was on bad terms with the clergy of Antioch, and the latin princes were eager to unite Cilicia with their dominions.

[7] There are some other matters, regarding the history of the Armenian kingdom in Cilicia, spoken of in the *Regesta Innocentii III.*; but it is not our object to write the history of that kingdom. We only collect materials for a future historian, who might certainly draw some other valuable accounts from *Belouacensis Spec. Hist.*, from *Sanutus* and from *Hayto* or *Hethum's Hist. Orient.* We may here observe, that Vahram, who is eager to tell all that is to the honour and glory of the Church, says nothing about the baptism of the great Chan of the Moguls.

[8] Leon was the first king, the former princes are only called barons of Cilicia.

Milton Keynes UK
Ingram Content Group UK Ltd.
UKHW030743071024
449371UK00006B/589

9 789362 095220